DIY HOMEMADE FACE MASKS

The Essential Quick Guide on How to Make Your Medical Face Mask at Home with Step-by-Step Process

DEDICATION

The author and publisher have provided this e-book to you for your personal use only. You may not make this e-book publicly available in any way. Copyright infringement is against the law. If you believe the copy of this e-book you are reading infringes on the author's copyright, please notify the publisher at: https://us.macmillan.com/piracy

Contents

What's the Best Material for a Mask?

Scientists are testing everyday items to find the best protection from coronavirus. Pillow cases, flannel pajamas and origami vacuum bags are all candidates.

Federal health officials have now recommended that we cover our faces with fabric during the coronavirus pandemic. But what material offers the most protection?

The Centers for Disease Control and Prevention has posted a no-sew mask pattern using a bandanna and a coffee filter as well as a video on making masks using rubber bands and folded fabrics found at home.

While a simple face covering can reduce the spread of coronavirus by blocking outgoing germs from coughs or sneezes of an infected person, experts say there is more variation in how much homemade masks might protect the wearer from incoming germs, depending on the fit and quality of the material used.

Scientists around the country have taken it upon themselves to identify everyday materials that do a better job of filtering microscopic particles. In recent tests, HEPA furnace filters scored well, as did vacuum cleaner bags, layers of 600-count pillowcases and fabric similar to flannel pajamas. Stacked coffee filters had medium scores. Scarves and bandanna material had the lowest scores, but still captured a small percentage of particles.

If you don't have any of the materials that were tested, a simple light test can help you decide whether a fabric is a good candidate for a mask.

“Hold it up to a bright light,” said Dr. Scott Segal, chairman of anesthesiology at Wake Forest Baptist Health who recently studied homemade masks. “If light passes really easily through the fibers and you can almost see the fibers, it’s not a good fabric. If it’s a denser weave of thicker material and light doesn’t pass through it as much, that’s the material you want to use.”

Researchers say it’s important to remember that lab studies are conducted under perfect conditions with no leaks or gaps in the mask, but the test methods give us a way to compare materials. And while the degree of filtration for some homemade masks seems low, most of us — who are staying home and practicing social distancing in public — don’t need the high level of protection required for medical workers. More important, any face covering is better than none, especially if worn by a person who has the virus but doesn’t know it.

The biggest challenge of choosing a homemade mask material is to find a fabric that is dense enough to capture viral particles, but breathable enough that we can actually wear it. Some items being touted online promise high filtration scores, but the material would be unwearable.

Yang Wang, an assistant professor of environmental engineering at Missouri University of Science and Technology, worked with his graduate students to study various combinations of layered materials — including both air filters and fabric. "You need something that is efficient for removing particles, but you also need to breathe," said Dr. Wang, who last fall won an international award for aerosol research.

To test everyday materials, scientists are using methods similar to those used to test medical masks, which everybody agrees should be saved for medical workers who are exposed to high doses of virus from seeing infected patients. The best medical mask — called the

N95 respirator — filters out at least 95 percent of particles as small as 0.3 microns. By comparison, a typical surgical mask — made using a rectangular piece of pleated fabric with elastic ear loops — has a filtration efficiency ranging from 60 to 80 percent.

Dr. Wang's group tested two types of air filters. An allergy-reduction HVAC filter worked the best, capturing 89 percent of particles with one layer and 94 percent with two layers. A furnace filter captured 75 percent with two layers, but required six layers to achieve 95 percent. To find a filter similar to those tested, look for a minimum efficiency reporting value (MERV) rating of 12 or higher or a microparticle performance rating of 1900 or higher.

The problem with air filters is that they potentially could shed small fibers that would be risky to inhale. So if you want to use a filter, you need to sandwich the filter between two layers of cotton fabric. Dr. Wang said one of his grad students made his own mask by following the instructions in the C.D.C. video, but adding several layers of filter material inside a bandanna.

Dr. Wang's group also found that when certain common fabrics were used, two layers offered far less protection than four layers. A 600 thread count pillow case captured just 22 percent of particles when doubled, but four layers captured nearly 60 percent. A thick woolen yarn scarf filtered 21 percent of particles in two layers, and 48.8 percent in four layers. A 100 percent cotton bandanna did the worst, capturing only 18.2 percent when doubled, and just 19.5 percent in four layers.

The group also tested Brew Rite and Natural Brew basket-style coffee filters, which, when stacked in three layers, showed 40 to 50 percent filtration efficiency — but they were less breathable than other options.

If you are lucky enough to know a quilter, ask them to make you a mask. Tests performed at the Wake Forest Institute for Regenerative Medicine in Winston-Salem, N.C., showed good results for homemade masks using quilting fabric. Dr. Segal, of Wake Forest Baptist Health, who led the study, noted that quilters tend to use high-quality, high-thread count cotton. The best homemade masks in his study were as good as surgical masks or slightly better, testing in the range of 70 to 79 percent filtration. Homemade masks that used flimsier fabric tested as low as 1 percent filtration, Dr. Segal said.

The best-performing designs were a mask constructed of two layers of high-quality, heavyweight "quilter's cotton," a two-layer mask made with thick batik fabric, and a double-layer mask with an inner layer of flannel and outer layer of cotton.

Bonnie Browning, executive show director for the American Quilter's Society, said that quilters prefer tightly woven cottons and batik fabrics that stand up over time. Ms. Browning said most sewing machines can handle only two layers of fabric when making a pleated mask, but someone who wanted four layers of protection could wear two masks at a time.

Ms. Browning said she recently reached out to quilters on Facebook and heard from 71 people who have made a combined total of nearly 15,000 masks. "We quilters are very much in the thick of what's going on with this," said Ms. Browning, who lives in Paducah, Ky. "One thing most of us have is a stash of fabric."

People who don't sew could try a folded origami mask, created by Jiangmei Wu, assistant professor of interior design at Indiana University. Ms. Wu, who is known for her breathtaking folded artwork, said she began designing a folded mask out of a medical and building material called Tyvek, as well as vacuum bags, after her brother in Hong Kong, where mask wearing is common, suggested it. (DuPont, the maker of Tyvek, said in a statement that Tyvek is intended for medical apparel, not masks.) The folded mask pattern is free online, as is a video demonstrating the folding process. In tests at Missouri University and University of Virginia, scientists found that vacuum bags removed between 60 percent and 87 percent of particles. But some brands of vacuum bags may contain fiberglass or are harder to breathe through than other materials, and shouldn't be used. Ms. Wu used a bag by EnviroCare Technologies, which has said it does not use fiberglass in its paper and synthetic cloth bags.

"I wanted to create an alternative for people who don't sew," said Ms. Wu, who said she is talking to various groups to find other materials that will be effective in a folded mask. "Given the shortage of all kinds of materials, even vacuum bags might run out."

The scientists who conducted the tests used a standard of 0.3 microns because that is the measure used by the National Institute for Occupational Safety and Health for medical masks.

Linsey Marr, a Virginia Tech aerosol scientist and an expert in the transmission of viruses, said the certification method for respirators and HEPA filters focuses on 0.3 microns because particles around that size are the hardest to catch. While it seems counterintuitive, particles smaller than 0.1 microns are actually easier to catch because they have a lot of random motion that makes them bump into the filter fibers, she said.

"Even though coronavirus is around 0.1 microns, it floats around in a wide range of sizes, from around 0.2 to several hundred microns, because people shed the virus in respiratory fluid droplets that also contain lots of salts and proteins and other things," said Dr. Marr. "Even if the water in the droplets fully evaporates, there's still a lot of salt and proteins and other gunk that stays behind as solid or gel-like material. I think 0.3 microns is still useful for guidance because the minimum filtration efficiency will be somewhere around this size, and it's what NIOSH uses."

How to Sew a Fabric Face Mask

Here's what you will need for this pattern:

Tools

- Needle and thread (and a sewing machine, if you have one)
- Scissors
- Pins or clips to hold fabrics in place (safety pins and paper clips will also work in a pinch)

Materials

- At least 20 by 20 inches of 100 percent cotton fabric, such as a flat tea towel (scroll to the end for more information about materials)
- 4 strips of cotton fabric for ties, about 18" long and ¾" wide

OR

- 4 flat, clean shoelaces

OR

- Two flat (1/4") sewing elastics that are 7" long each

Choose your piece of cotton fabric, pre-wash it on the warmest setting and dry it on high heat. (Tea towels are better to use than T-shirts or linens, according to the Stanford Anesthesia Informatics and Media Lab.)

Fold the fabric in half. Measure and cut out a 9.5" by 6.5" rectangle to create two identically sized layers. This is your mask base.

Now it's on to the fabric ties.

Cut 4 thin pieces of material, about 18" long and ¾" wide. Fold each piece of fabric twice lengthwise, then once more to tuck the rough edges inside. Sew a straight line along the middle. This will prevent the fabric ties from having frayed edges.

Step 2:

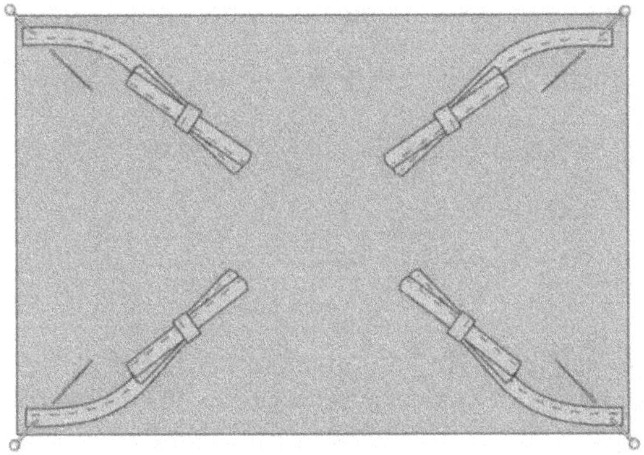

Take one of your rectangular fabric layers. With the "right side" (or the outer-facing side, where the pattern might be) facing you, pin down the 4 fabric ties, one piece per corner. Make sure that the ties are gathered in the center of the fabric layer before advancing to the next step.

You can also substitute sewing elastic for fabric ties, but note that elastic cannot be bleached (and therefore, is not as easy to clean) and that anyone with a latex allergy cannot wear it. (Elastic is also increasingly in short supply.) Attach elastics to the first layer of fabric by securing the ends at the corners, forming little hoops. Make sure the elastic lies inside the perimeter of your fabric.

Step 3

Take the second layer of fabric and line it up with the first. The "right sides" (or patterned sides) of the fabric should be facing each other, sandwiching the fabric ties or elastics. Secure the fabric sandwich together with pins.

Step 4

Eyeball a midway point. From the middle, sew a straight line across the mask, about ¼" above the bottom edge of the fabric, toward the bottom left-hand corner. Remove any pins as you sew past them.

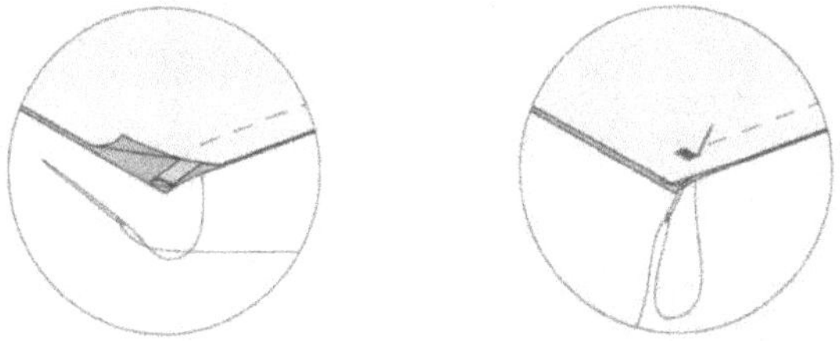

Make sure that the elastic or fabric ties are secured in the corners, sandwiched by your two layers of fabric, as you sew over their ends. You want to make sure your needle goes through the three pieces: the top layer, the end of the fabric tie, and the bottom layer. Add a couple stitches forward and backward (in both directions) to secure your ties in place.

Step 5

Stitch all around the perimeter of the fabric layers, repeating the forward and backward motion at each corner to secure all the elastic ends or fabric ties.

Continue to stitch your way toward the starting point, but stop to allow for a 1 ½" gap.

Step 6

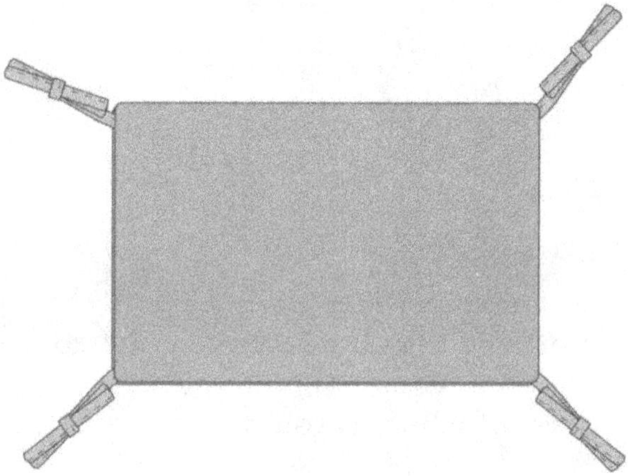

Turn your project right-side out from the little 1 ½" gap. Your fabric ties or elastics should now stick out, like little legs.

Step 7

Make three staggered pleats lengthwise on the mask, as if folding a paper fan. This helps the mask conform to the wearer's face. Secure each pleat with pins.

Step 8

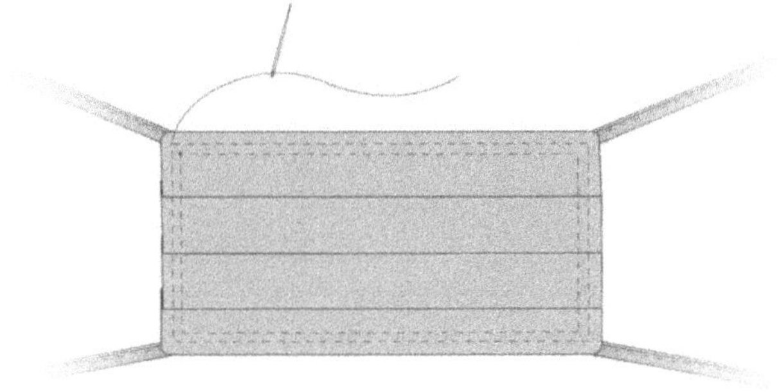

With your pleats held in place by pins, stitch around the perimeter of the mask, ¼" away from the edge of the seam. This is called a top stitch. Take care when stitching over the pleats as the fabric may be quite thick.

Top stitch a second time around, about ¼" in from the first round of stitching. Now you have a completed mask.

Next up? Learning to wear a mask correctly is important. Many people pull them aside, hampering their effect, and also air can get in easily around the edges.

Stitching Scientist Pleated Face Mask

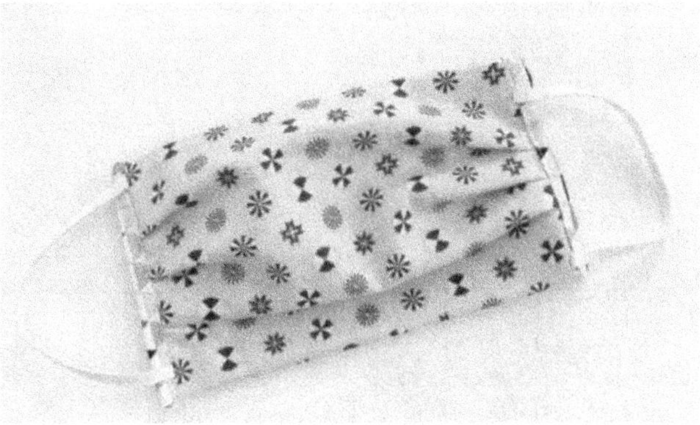

Materials

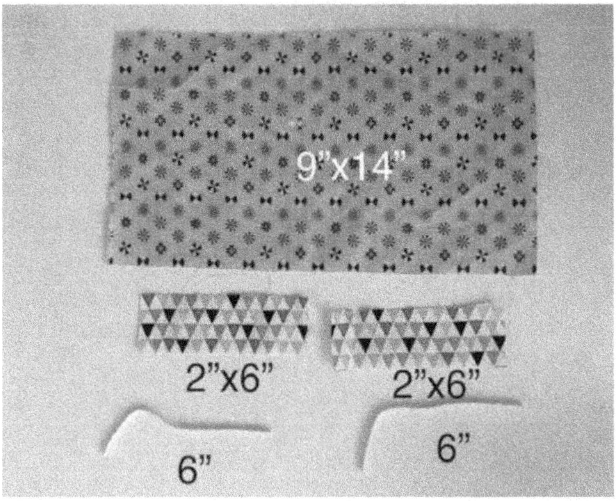

Start Sewing

Step 1 - Fold main fabric right side together on the long side Sew. Turn inside out and iron.

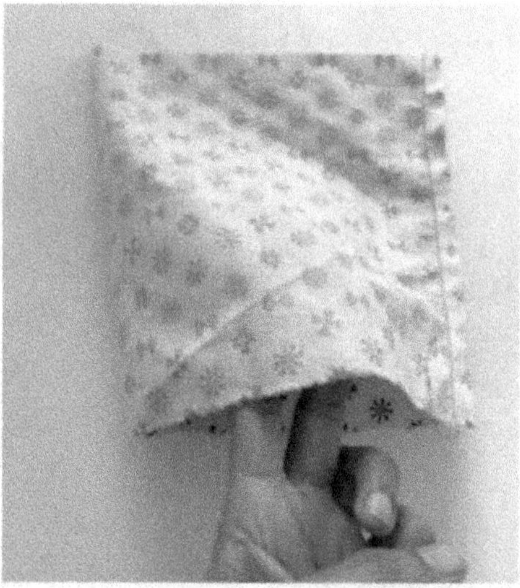

Step 2a. Fold inwards about 1" to form pleats on the short side of the fabric.

Step 2b - Form 3 pleats on each side. Pin down

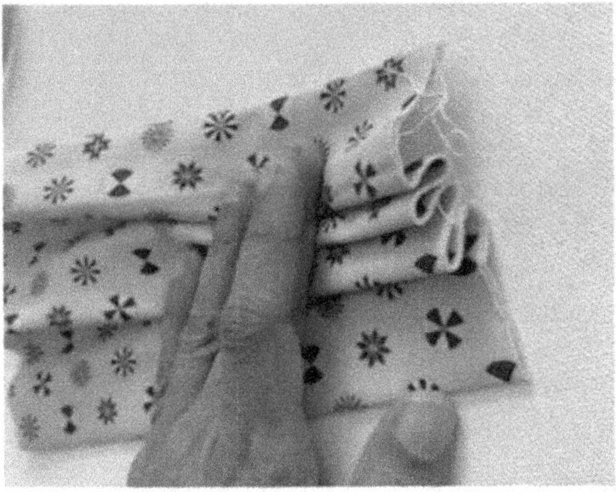

Step 3 - Sew the sides straight down

Step 4 - Sew elastic inwards on both sides

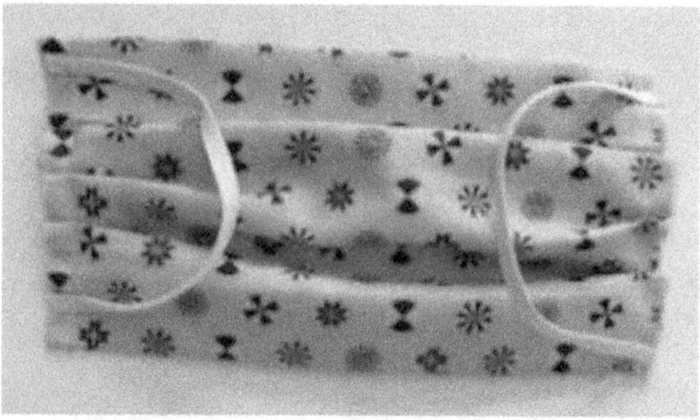

Step 5 - Fold side pieces half way on short side and iron down

Step 6 - Line up raw edge of side piece to raw edge of main piece.

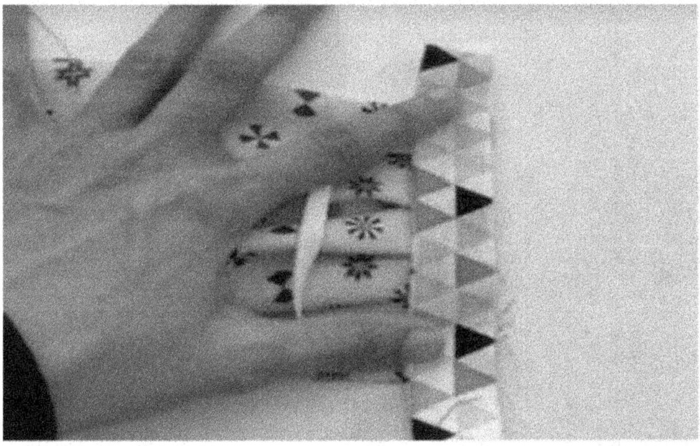

Step 7 - Fold over the ends of the side piece on the back of the mask. Pin

Step 8 - Sew on the front side of the side piece.

Step 9 - Fold over the side piece and sew down. Repeat for other side.

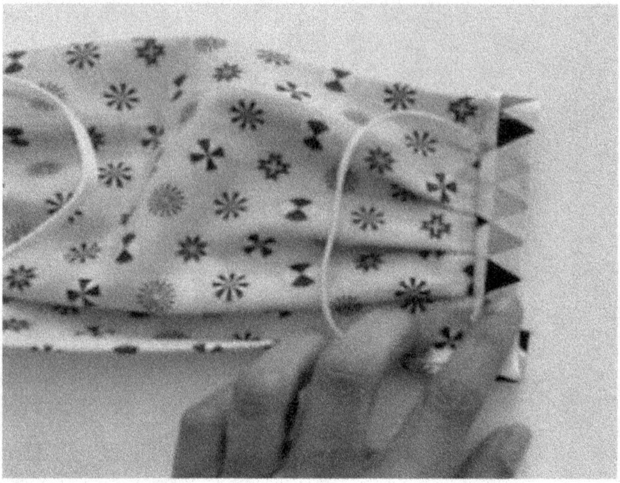

Oita Japan DIY 3D Homemade Mask

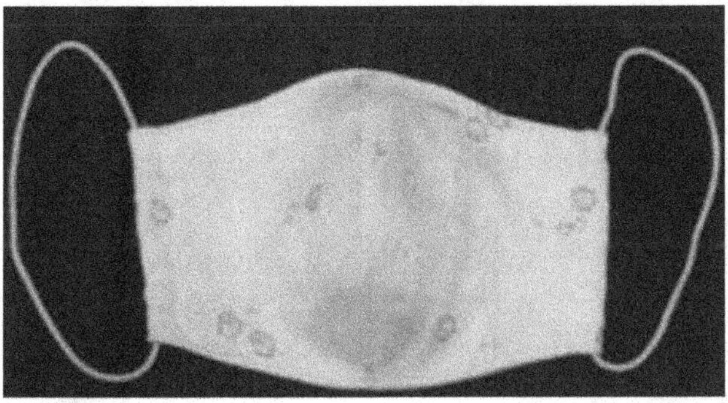

Materials

- Gauze fabric 18*22cm (x2)
- (Mask shown in sample image is made from a patterned material)
- Gauze handkerchiefs or gauze towels can be used as substitutes
- Elastic bands for masks (x2)
- TEKNOROTE (elastic chord for shape-holding) 9cm (x1)

Method

1. Lay the fabric pieces on top of each other, then sew 1cm away from the seam
allowance on the top and bottom (22cm) sides.
2. Flip the fabrics inside out so the threads are hidden, then sew 0.8cm away from the
seam allowance on both the top and bottom sides.
3. On the top side (i.e. the side with the 0.8cm and 1cm stitches), measure 4.5cm from
the centre and make a stitch perpendicular to and in-between the two existing
stitches.
4. Thread the elastic chord through the top side, then make another stitch to secure
the chord in the center.
5. Fold the fabric down in half so the top and bottom sides face each other. Measure
3cm above the center fold and make a 0.8cm mountain fold, then measure 2.5cm

below the center fold and make another 0.8cm mountain fold. Iron the folds to hold
them in place.

6. Make three stitches along both of the shorter sides, 0.2cm, 1cm and 2cm from the
seam allowance. Cut away any excess threads.

7. Fold both sides of the mask inward twice, then make a stitch 2cm away from both
edges to hold all the folds in place.

8. Thread the elastic straps through the sides and make two individual loops.

*Adjust the length of the straps to your personal preference.

No-sew Face Mask DIY

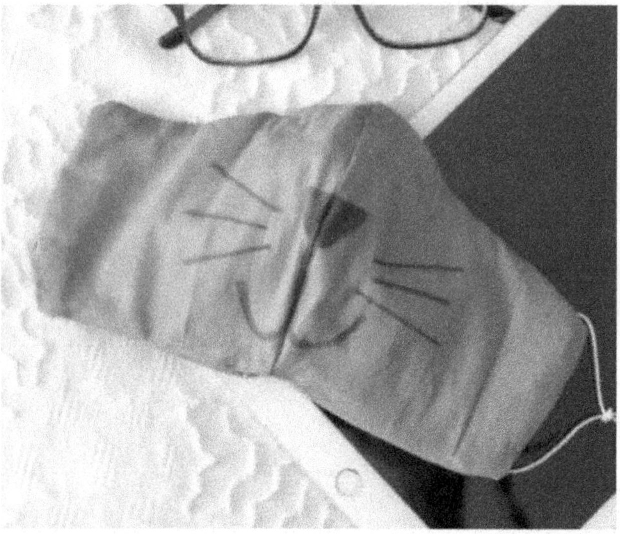

Supplies:

- 100% cotton fabric, tightly woven and pre-washed
- Lightweight fusible interfacing
- Thin elastic
- Aleene's Fabric Fusion Glue
- Scissors
- Tulip Rainbow Fabric Markers

- Free Surgical Face Mask Template

Step 1: Cut 4 mask shapes from the fabric. Then cut 2 from the interfacing.

Step 2: Take 2 fabric mask shapes and arrange them with the curved ends away from each other. Add Aleene's Fabric Fusion Glue to all edges and place the interfacing on top. Press down to adhere. Then flip the pieces over.

Step 3: With right sides of the fabric together, glue the pieces together along the curved edge only. Let dry.

Step 4: Place right sides of the un-lined fabric pieces together. Glue together at the curved edge and let dry.

Step 5: Once dry enough to manipulate, turn both pieces right side out.

Step 6: Place the right sides of the fabric pieces together. With the curved part of the mask at the top, insert the elastic pieces in each side, making sure they are encased inside the mask. See above photo for placement. Then glue all the way around, with the exception of about 3 inches at the bottom. Let dry for about 4 hours until secure.

Step 7: Turn the no-sew face mask right side out through the hole in the mask. Then fold the opening inward and glue in place. Hold in place with a paperclip if needed.

Step 8: Once dry, get to decorating! Use the Tulip fabric markers to draw on the mask, or utilize stencils.

Based on how the no-sew face mask fits the owner, you/they may want to tie loops in the elastic ear pieces for a more snug fit. Make multiple for friends, family and even grocery store workers who don't have access to supplies right now. Please note that the internal interfacing can deteriorate over several washes.

Times like this bring out both the best and worst of people. I'm thankful to see the best in many of my fellow makers.

DIY no sew face mask similar to the N95 face mask

WHAT IS SO SPECIAL ABOUT THE N95 MASK?

For starters, the N95 respiratory masks are very effective in filtering or blocking very small particles in the air that are transmitted by coughs and sneezes (unlike surgical masks). This makes them a good choice to protect against highly contagious viruses.

WHAT DO THE N95 MASKS LOOK LIKE?

Below is a picture of an old N95 mask that I have.

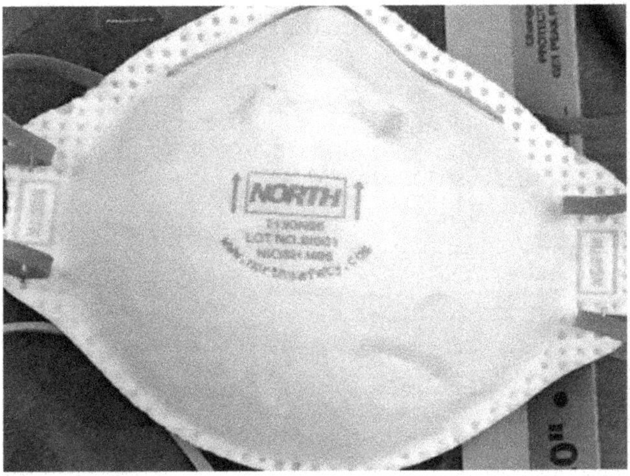

They are designed to fit close to the face and block out 95% of small particles (hence the name N95). Most of the diagrams I've seen show 4 different layers, one being a filter. You can see an example of a N95 mask below from Softseal Respirator mask.

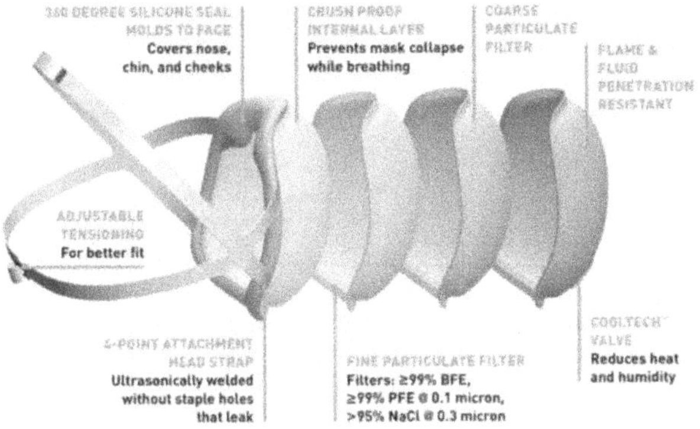

MATERIALS to create your own homemade protective face mask similar to an N95 mask

- AC Air Filter – make sure it's not fiberglass
- Fabric
- Scissors
- Fabric tape
- Elastic or rubber bands
- Hot glue gun
- Wire clothes hanger
- Pliers or wire cutters
- Stapler

HOW TO MAKE

1. Create a stencil- I did this by tracing the old N95 mask I had. Don't forget to add an inch or two inches all the way around. I've shared my stencil below.
2. Double up the fabric and trace the stencil over the fabric.

3. Cut 4 pieces of fabric.
4. Trace your stencil over the AC filter and cut it out.
5. Hot glue one layer of fabric to the AC filter.
6. Hot glue another layer.
7. Cut two pieces of wire from the clothes hanger about 5" each
8. Bend the two pieces slightly to match the angle of the pattern on the top and the bottom.
9. Hot glue the wire pieces to the top and bottom INSIDE piece of fabric (the bottom piece of fabric).
10. Hot glue all around the face mask to make sure it's sealed.
11. Use your fingers to pinch the sides and hot glue them together (see video for more details).
12. Cut 2 elastic or rubber bands to fit your face.
13. Staple them to the OUTSIDE of the mask on each side. One needs to extend above your ears and one below.
14. Take the last piece of fabric and pinch the sides and hot glue it together.

15. Use the fabric tape to tape the last piece of fabric to the mask.

DIY DUST MASK TEMPLATE

One thing to note about N95 masks is that most of them have four layers and at least one of those layers is considered a "filter."

I figured the "filter" layer could be created from an extra AC filter I had. Why not right? It's kind of the same principal.

Let me show you some how-to pictures:

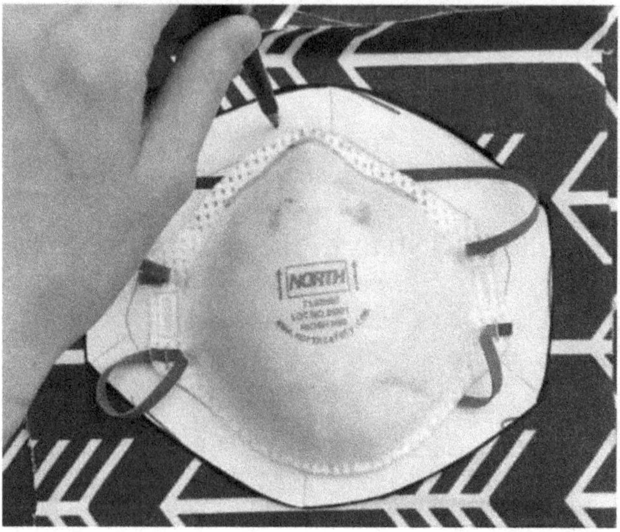

Make a template with an existing mask (use my template if you don't have one)

Trace the template onto the fabric

Next use the stencil to cut the AC filter. Make sure you don't use a fiberglass filter.

Cut out the fabric- you need 3 pieces (more if you want extras)

You can see the metal pieces I've cut from the clothes hanger.

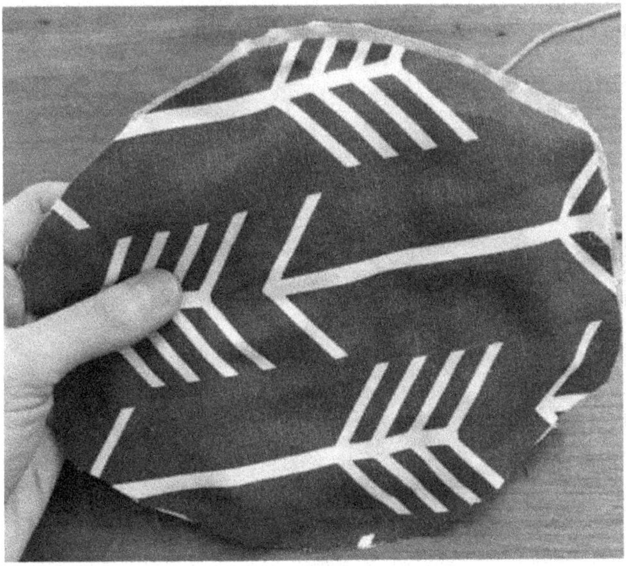

What it looks like after it's glued together

Pinch the sides to create a molded look

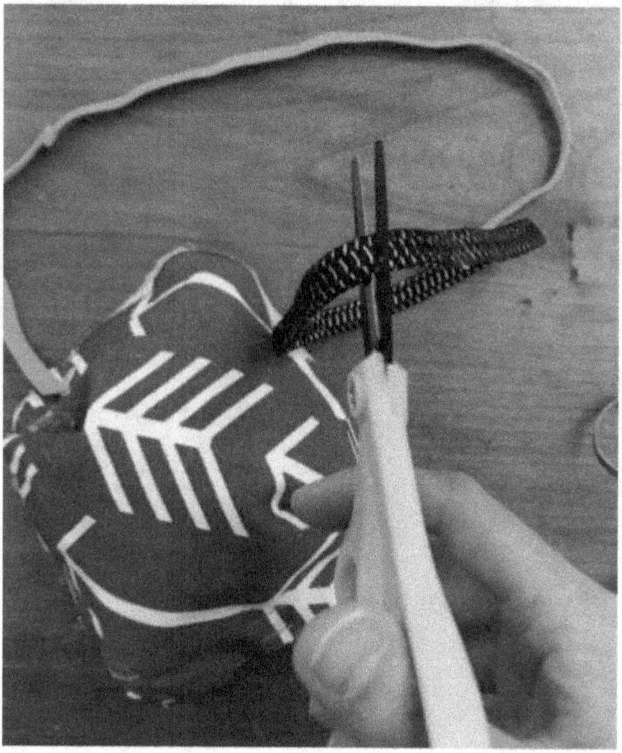

Cut the bands to fit and staple them to the mask

Attach fabric tape to the back of the extra piece of fabric

YOUR DIY MASK WILL INCLUDE FOUR LAYERS:

1. base fabric layer that sits on your face
2. AC filter cut to size
3. another fabric layer on top of AC filter
4. "disposable" fabric layer attached with either fabric tape or velcro

How To Make A 5 Minute Face Mask

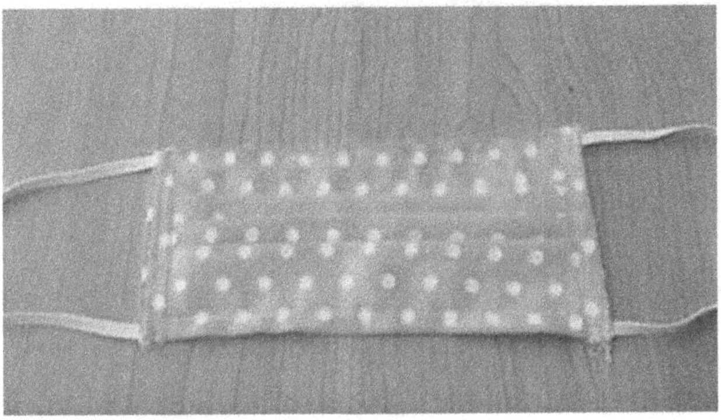

Materials Needed

- Scissors
- Thread
- Small piece of Fabric (cut 20 x 17)
- Elastic (for the earpieces)
- A Sewing Machine

Step One:

First, Cut Your Fabric Into A Rectangle Shape (20 X 17).

Then Fold Over And Sew Down The Edges, Then Make Pleats So The Mask Is Expandable.

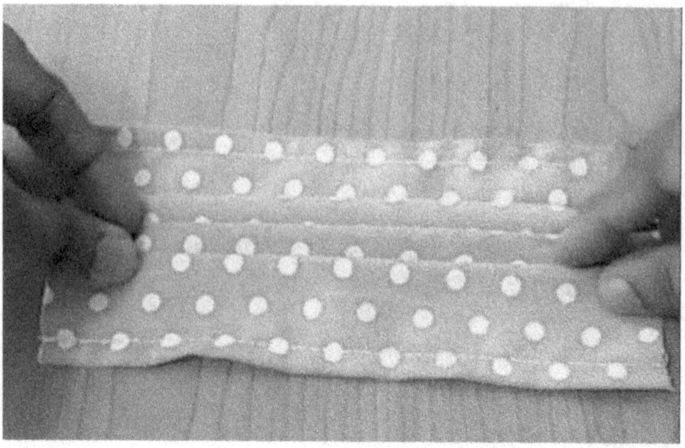

Then Sew The Elastic (15 Cm) On Each Side To Hold The DIY Face Mask Over Your Ears.

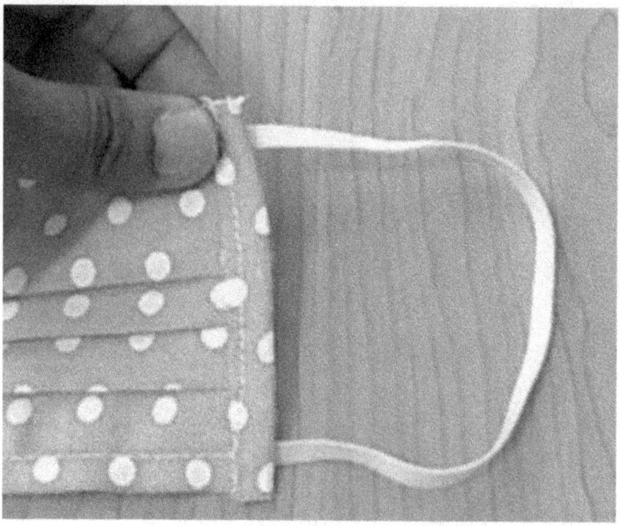

Please note: This mask can not prevent Covid-19 nor will it protect as much as an N-95 respirator mask. The tutorial for this fabric mask and info in this article is provided for educational and entertainment purposes only. For more information on Covid-19, please visit the CDC website which states "In settings where facemasks are not available, HCP (healthcare personnel) might use homemade masks (e.g., bandana, scarf) for care of patients with COVID-19 as a last resort. However, homemade masks are not considered PPE, since their capability to protect HCP is unknown. Caution should be exercised when considering this option. Homemade masks should ideally be used in combination with a face shield that covers the entire front (that extends to the chin or below) and sides of the face."

How to add nose wire to face masks

Now if you really want masks to fit well, or if you have glasses, then adding nose wire is a must. Nose bridge wire keeps my mask from slipping down my face. I'll show you three ways how to add nose wire to face masks: (1) adhesive nose bridge wire, (2) sewing wire into the mask while you're making it, (3) adding wire to purchased or finished masks.

Option 1: Adhesive nose bridge wire

An easy no-sew option is to attach adhesive nose bridge wire to the outside of your mask; the adhesive tends to last several washings before needing to swap out a new one. Fortunately, this pack of 100 adhesive nose bridge wires is low priced.

Option 2: Sew wire into the mask while you're making it

This option is easy when sewing masks yourself. Just slip the wire inside the mask and sew into the seam allowance about 2" from the side.

I prefer these wide nose bridge wires. Sew a little "pocket" (see the image below) to add these wide nose bridge wires inside the mask which I think is a bit more comfortable than thin silver wire. Below, you can see the pocket where I slipped the wider nose bridge in, then sew the end shut so it's secured permanently. If you do use thin silver wire then be sure to bend the ends into little circles using these wire cutters to avoid pokes.

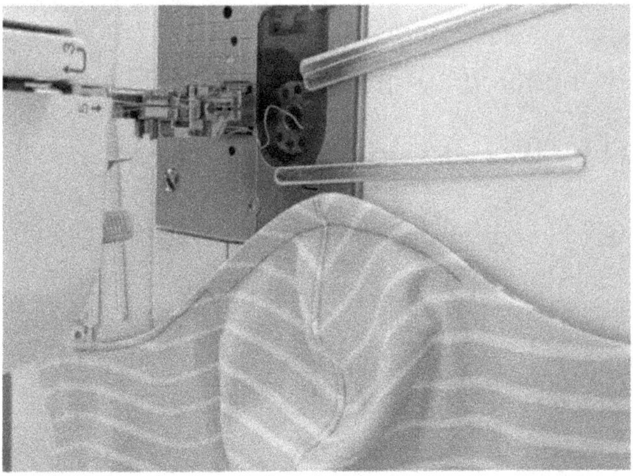

Option 3: Add nose wire to purchased masks (or after masks are sewn)

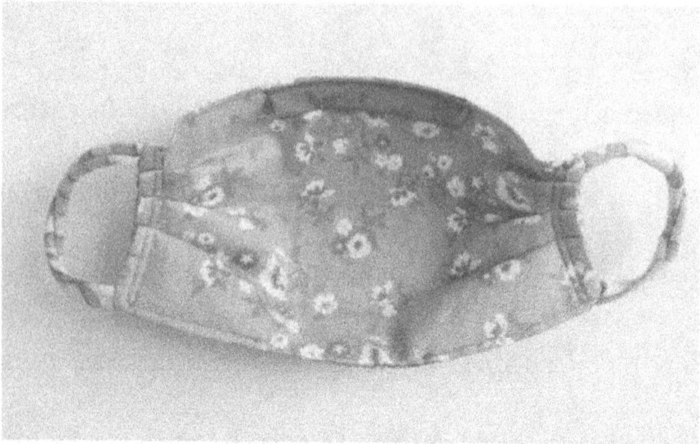

This option is good for adding nose wire to purchased masks. You can use these wide nose bridge wires which personally I prefer, or you can use thin silver wire and cut and bend it using these wire cutters. Below I'm showing the thin wire sticking out a little bit so that you can see how I bent the ends into little circles to avoid pokes. Normally, the nose wire will be totally inside the casing before sewing it in.

I'll show you Option 3 in detail below…

How to add nose wire to purchased masks

Step 1: Cut and sew bias tape (or a strip of folded fabric) onto the top inside of the face mask

I sewed 4" of bias tape on the top inside of the mask. Use 1/4" bias tape for thin silver wire and 1/2" bias tape for wide nose bridge wires. No bias tape? Then just cut a rectangle of fabric 4" x 2" to make your own 1/2" casing (fold it in half, iron, then fold raw edges into the center, iron). Center the bias tape onto the top edge of your mask and pin or clip. Make sure the open edges of the bias tape are on the top edge of the mask, like the photo below; the folded edge of the bias tape should be on the bottom.

Then sew the bias tape along its open edge to secure it to the mask and close the open edges of the bias tape. If you used 1/2" bias tape, then be sure to also sew the bottom edge to secure it. I am showing 1/4" bias tape below.

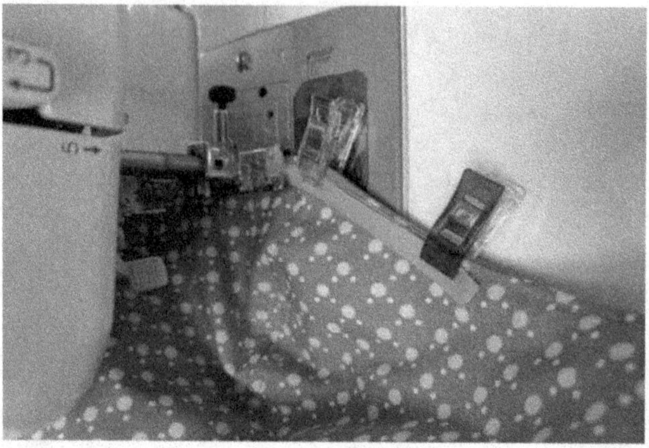

Step 2: Cut a piece of nose wire and insert into the casing

Slip in a piece of removable floral wire / twist ties / pipe cleaner / opened paper clip. Below, I'm showing the thin silver wire that I cut and bent using these wire cutters. Curve both ends of the wire so they won't poke you when wearing the mask. To sew the wire in permanently (so that it's not removable) then sew both ends shut after inserting the wire to permanently encase the wire in the mask.

Here's what the nose wire casing looks like inside of the pleated-style face mask using thin silver wire:

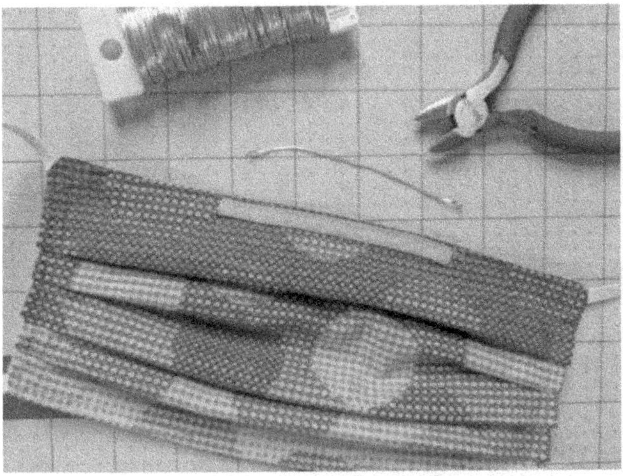

Step 3: Put on the face mask and bend the wire to fit your nose

Here's what the nose wire will look like once it's fully inside the face mask. Put on the face mask and bend the nose wire to better fit your nose.

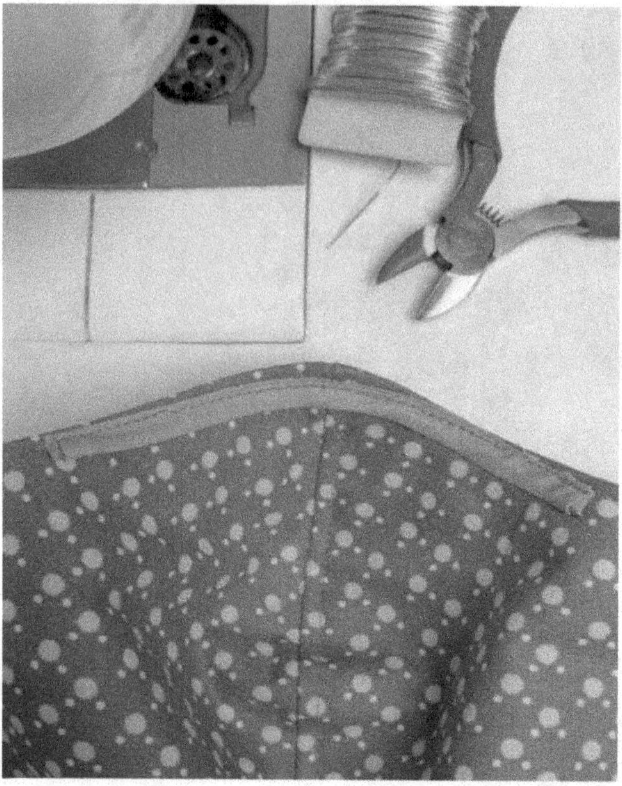

Tips when sewing DIY face masks for kids

Making kids' masks involved some trial and error to balance what my kids would be willing to wear and what stayed on best. Here's my advice for making kids masks:

1. Use soft knit ties rather than thick elastic.

My kids (ages 7 and 10) greatly prefer the knit ties to elastic for both ear loop and behind-the-head ties that we tie into a bow. You could try elastic for around-the-head kids face mask; my kids just didn't like the feel of elastic. Here are the knit ties that I use on masks, or you can make your own from old t-shirts or knit fabric by cutting 1" wide strips and pulling them until they curl. You could also try ribbon, fabric ties, or shoestrings.

If you'd like to try elastic, then I recommend using this round cord elastic for soft ear loops. The nice thing about using this round cord elastic is that you can add these silicone cord stops to the ear loops so that you can adjust the mask to fit better behind your child's ears. Neat trick, yes?

2. Consider age and activity level when choosing ear loops vs. behind-the-head fastening.

My kids have pleated and smooth masks, some with ear loops, some with behind-the-head ties. For my kids, it seems that the around-the-head ties have stayed on best (compared with the earloop style) but consider your child's age and activity level. We tend to choose to wear the ear loop style for walks and the behind-the-head style for greater physical activity.

For pleated kids masks: For my kids (age 10 and 7), cutting one piece of fabric 7" wide x 12" tall and folding it half worked for them. I use two 6" earloops for ear loop styles.

3. Add nose wire to kids' masks.

It's best to avoid kids touching their masks while wearing them to adjust their fit. Adding nose wire to kids' masks helped them fit my kids better. I use this these wide nose bridge wires on kid's masks but you can also use thin silver wire.

Below are my 1o-year-old's daughter's smooth-style face masks. This one uses behind-the-head knit ties using the Craft Passion style to allow it to fit snugly on the top & bottom and tied it into a bow (note that the smooth mask but also works with ear loops).

How to Wash Masks

How to clean:

Washing machine

You can include your mask with your regular laundry.

Use regular laundry detergent and the warmest appropriate water setting for the cloth used to make the mask.

Washing by hand

1. Check the label to see if your bleach is intended for disinfection. Some bleach products, such as those designed for safe use on colored clothing, may not be suitable for disinfection.

- Use bleach containing 5.25%–8.25% sodium hypochlorite. Do not use a bleach product if the percentage is not in this range or is not specified.
- Ensure the bleach product is not past its expiration date. Never mix household bleach with ammonia or any other cleanser.
- Ensure adequate ventilation.

2. Prepare a bleach solution by mixing:

- 5 tablespoons (1/3rd cup) of 5.25%–8.25% bleach per gallon of room temperature water or
- 4 teaspoons of 5.25%–8.25% bleach per quart of room temperature water

3. Soak the mask in the bleach solution for 5 minutes.

4. Discard the bleach solution down the drain and rinse the mask thoroughly with cool or room temperature water.

5. Make sure to completely dry the mask after washing.

How to dry

Dryer

Use the highest heat setting and leave in the dryer until completely dry.

Illustration clothes in dryer

Air dry

Lay flat and allow to completely dry. If possible, place the mask in direct sunlight.

CPSIA information can be obtained
at www.ICGtesting.com
Printed in the USA
LVHW111558221120
672387LV00007B/1546

9 798566 230412